Coding Games for ___

A Step-by-Step Guide and Creative Activities in
Scratch for Creating Animations and Games

By

Kangaroo Publications

Jesse Broome

TABLE OF CONTENTS

Introduction

If you are a kid and you are reading this book by yourself, you may need an adult with you for some help. I know, kids like to explore the technology on their own, but you might need help in installing Scratch on your PC, so that you can start doing your own magic. If you are an adult, your kid might need your help. So, just hang around with your kids and help them learn this fantastic stuff.

Scratch is a fantastic tool that allows a kid or any beginner, create a video animation, project, and games. Scratch is a programming language that helps your kid develop social and emotional skills. It gives an entertaining and vibrant environment where you can learn through different interactive projects. Using Scratch, a kid can quickly learn how to make media-rich content such as games, animations, reports, etc. Scratch has been designed to enable you to access options that only a professional programmer could use. This user-friendly programming language has a wide range of tools (especially multimedia ones), so you can make many different applications. The best thing about Scratch is that it is way more accessible since it is simpler to use. We can say that Scratch is a booster for developing your problem-solving skills too, and not only for programming but for many other aspects of life.

Scratch programming has been designed with a very intuitive user interface that gives additional fun to the program's learning process. It is effortless and well-suited as an educational tool for children, students, and anyone interested in learning programming. The beauty of learning programming with Scratch is that the Scratch learning process is easy to understand, whether or not you have any prior knowledge of programming.

In today's world, kids need to identify and hone their creative side. It will immensely help them grow up and look up to do mature things, such as finding a job. Our world is changing fast, and the professional skills of the past are becoming obsolete every day. Everything is being automated, day-to-day management and operational jobs are getting scarce, and it will worsen when the kids grow up. But, do you know what machines won't be? Humans!

What is Human Creativity? The mind, the feelings, the heart, and the things that make us human!

Every kid is different. Some might find this book surprising, while some might not be interested in coding. It is entirely understandable, and the idea of this book is to fuel the creative mind and spark a response.

Programming is no different from reading and writing. All it takes is practice and a guiding hand to help you through the frustrating parts.

In this Scratch Programming Guide, you will learn the fundamental concepts behind programming, and you will understand step-by-step everything from installing Python to developing games. You will start by preparing your work environment and acquiring every tool you need. Then you will learn what variables are, how functions are created, and why loops and conditional statements can make programs so intelligent.

This e-book is a comprehensive guide on using Scratch programming language to create educative and exciting animations, interactive stories, and games using the impressive dragging and dropping block format embedded in the programming process. All the projects examined in this book guide you into becoming an excellent programmer.

Chapter 1: Welcome to Scratch Programming

1.1 Knowing more about Scratch

What is Scratch Programming?

Scratch is a programming language designed by Technology's Kindergarten group of the Massachusetts Institute. Scratch is more like lego blocks, so we may call it a block-based graphical computer programming language. You can animate stories, games, art; even you can add music in all the previously mentioned disciplines. Scratch is a global programming language translated into more than seventy languages. Programmers name Scratch, a programming equivalent of LEGO.

Now! Isn't this MAGIC?

Have you ever attended a Disc Jokey concert? They use a technique of combining different kinds of music, which is known as scratching. Scripting can mix two different records and produce various sound effects and different types of music. So, the name "Scratch" originated from the DJ's scratching technique.

Similar to the scratching technique, Scratch programming can creatively combine various media types, such as sounds, images, diagrams, etc., to create something unique and new. Like Scratching, Scratch programmers combined different media (image, sounds, diagrams, and many more) in a very creative way and developed something entirely new and unique.

Who Is Scratch for?

When Scratch programming was first launched, its primary aim was to enable children aged 8 to16 to learn programming language quickly. However, whether 8 or 80, Scratch programming is available for everybody irrespective of age or color. Younger children with their parents can enjoy learning to program with Scratch; however, older men or women could also start their journey into learning programming language with Scratch.

Also, the performance level of anyone learning to program with Scratch would not be slowed down by their keyboard skills or the inability to operate complex codes. Working with Scratch involves the use of dragging and dropping code blocks. This technique helps to minimize the typing needed to create any design.

Since Scratch can efficiently run on a user's website, installing any software is unnecessary. Aside from this, it is impossible for Scratch programming to harm or damage the files stored on your computer. The program is free, and it does not have any inbuilt ads or in-app purchases, allowing for a dedicated and enjoyable learning process.

Scratch makes programming an entertaining and exciting ordeal. It does not have any error messages that pop up and confuse you when the program is going on. Neither does it have any unnecessary redirection messages.

Also, with the Scratch user's account, a user can share any of their projects with the scratch community when online. This advantage gives you a sense of community and the feeling of interacting with a whole audience. As a result, many schools have included Scratch programming in their curriculum.

Why Is Scratch Ideal for Beginners?

The simplicity of Scratch has made it a go-to for beginners in programming. Other programming languages like Ruby, PHP, Java, and even Python are difficult to learn. However, starting with any of these can bring one or two difficulties, especially in understanding the technicalities. With Scratch, the most important thing needed is the desire to learn. With or without using PowerPoint or OpenOffice.org effectively, you would find support and flow smoothly with the Scratch programming process.

Scratch building-block approaches are effortless; as a result, after using it for a while, advancing in other programming languages would become very easy.

Scratch offers a fantastic opportunity for anyone interested in learning programming. Since a learner does not necessarily need to know how this works, its advantages are all-encompassing.

Here are a few benefits of learning with Scratch:

1. The most evident and widespread use of Scratch is to teach children, students, or yourself how to program.
2. Scratch can be used to illustrate mathematical terms. A good example is the use of Scratch to set up interactive games, especially games that use variables to keep track of their scores or rotate on the variable data.
3. With the storytelling ability of Scratch, it can help instill a reading thirst in children and improve adults' reading ability. Scratch can be used to convert an essay, especially a persuasive essay, into a Scratch project.
4. It improves a child's creative genius. This can be done by encouraging your child to create a Scratch video, especially if they like video games.

There are three major types of Scratch programming, and they are Scratch 1.4, scratch 2.0, and scratch 3.0

1.2 An Overview of Scratch Blocks

We will use this section to talk more about the blocks available in Scratch. You will learn more about their names and their role in the program. The purpose is to define terms that might be unknown to you, and that will be used throughout this guide. This part of the guide can be a part that you will return to whenever you feel stuck, and you need to remind yourself of certain expressions. The version of Scratch that we use as a reference in the guide offers four types of blocks. These blocks are the Function Blocks, the Command Blocks, the Control Blocks, and the Trigger Blocks.

The Control Blocks and the Command Blocks are also known as the Stacks. They have notches on their tops or puzzle like structures on their bottoms. These blocks can be snapped together into the stacks as their name suggests.

Functions and Arithmetic Operators in Scratch

In this section, we will cover the most important things you need to understand about the functions and arithmetic operations Scratch supports. If you, for example, need to calculate something and do not have a calculator anywhere around, you can just make one using the program by means of the blocks from the operators' palette.

The operators' palette offers blocks that can perform all four basic arithmetic operations. Whether you want to multiply, add, subtract, or divide numbers, you can do that by running these blocks. Since they produce numbers, they can be used as inputs for all other blocks that support numeric values.

Scratch supports the basic operations and the modulus operator (mod), which allows you to return the remainder of the two numbers' division. For instance, if you put 10mod3, the return is one because when you divide ten by three, the rest of these two numbers is number 1. The most common usage of this operator is when you want to test if one whole number (or integer) is divisible by other smaller numbers. If the modulus is 0, the more significant number can be divided with a lower number. Modulus allows you to see if the number you will get is even or odd. Additionally, Scratch also supports round operator, which has the purpose of rounding decimals to the nearest number that is whole. For example, if you get 3.1, the round operator will round it to the number 3. If the number is 2.6, the round operator will round it to 3, and so forth.

When you start using Scratch more often, at some point, you will need to know how to generate random numbers. This is especially important if you want to create more games or simulations. Scratch has random blocks that are designed specifically for that. Random blocks create outputs, which are, as their name suggests, random numbers each time you click on them. These blocks have editable white areas inside where you can enter a range for the number you need. Scratch will always choose the number between the values you have set, including them. Keep in mind that you will get different outputs if you set ending values to be 1 to 2 or 1 to 1.0. If you choose the first version, you will get the whole numbers, which are, in this case, 1 or 2. Still, if you select the other version, the random pick will be a decimal value between 1 and 2. Whenever you set a decimal number as the limiting input, the output you get will also be a decimal.

Other than these basic operations, Scratch can support various mathematical functions. If you put different blocks together, the program can perform up to 14 mathematical functions in the drop menu. Some of these functions are logarithms and trigonometry, calculating the square root of a number, or finding the exponential function. If you want to learn more about this Scratch feature, the best thing is to use the Mathematical Functions manual found in the program's support documents. This file contains more extensive coverage of all functions that you can perform in Scratch and how to combine blocks.

You had the opportunity to read more about the different elements of the web user interface, and we will even talk about the complete process of making a game. Through these previous sections, you could explore using Scratch to build your calculator that can support different operations and functions. At this point, we are clear that you are familiar with the most basic information that you need to make some more complicated scripts. Still, it is a long way before you can write advanced programs. In the next chapter, we will talk more about some skills that will improve your programming ability in Scratch, but before that, here are a few examples that you can use to practice the things you have learned so far.

Firstly, you can view the mathematical operations like 8x8, 88x88, 888x888, etc., and determine if there is a pattern in these functions. To check your answers, use the "say" command and calculate the results with Scratch.

The third task that you can do to check how Scratch operates with math functions is to try calculating values like the sine of 60°, for example, or the square root of 45, and then check if those values are the same in Scratch when you run the "say" command. You can also try rounding some numbers or creating functional blocks to calculate the average of numbers like 80, 85, 88, etc. You will use the "say" command to display the result each time.

If you want to try some more complicated tasks, you can create function blocks that will convert Fahrenheit to Celsius. Let's say that you want to convert 70 Fahrenheit into Celsius. Keep in mind that:

$$Celsius = (5/9) \times (Fahrenheit - 32)$$

You can try creating function blocks that will calculate the area of a trapezoid. Let's say that the height of that trapezoid is 5/7 feet and that the basis of the trapezoid has lengths of 4/8 and 21/8 feet. Remember that the formula should be A= 0.5 x (b1 +b2) x h. In this case, b1 and b2 refer to the lengths of the basis, and h refers to the height of the trapezoid.

If you want to create blocks that involve formulas from physics rather than just math, you can try creating a function block that will calculate the force that you would need to accelerate a 2.300kg car 4m/s2.

Reminder: the formula for calculating the force is mass multiplied with acceleration.

1.3 Installing and Setting up

Scratch can be used in two ways:

- As an Online platform (You do not need to install)
- As an Offline Version of Scratch (You can install Scratch onto your PC)

The Online Scratch

The link to the Scratch website is

https://scratch.mit.edu/

Simply, open your web browser, and go to this link. Scratch's website will look like the below-mentioned screenshot.

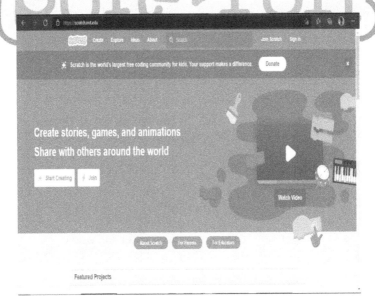

If you want to start your projects online, you may click "Create."

Account creation will allow you to share your projects with other programmers and make online friends in a safe community. You just need to click on "Join Scratch" to create your Scratch account. The best thing is that it is free.

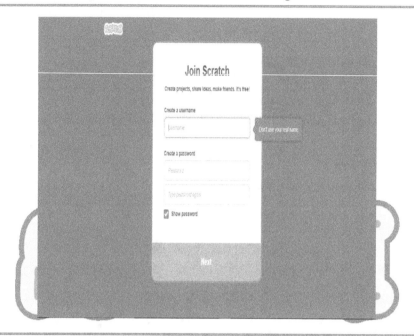

Offline Application (Preferred)

In the offline version, you do not have to sign up for an account to use the Scratch application on your computer. The downside is that you will not be able to share your projects with others on the Internet.

Hey kid, good news, no more adults, and we are all set up to have fun! I have to ask you a question. Do you know who Peter Pan is? Yes? Good job, smarty-pants. Let me tell you anyway because I also have a secret to share.

Peter Pan is an independent, confident, free-spirited kid who can fly, do magic stuff, goes on adventures, helps other kids, and stands against evil. He's also a bit naughty, which is good, right? He also leads other kids to be good and have fun.

The saddest part is that everyone thinks Peter Pan is not real.

But I know a secret no one else does, and I can't hold onto it any longer. Let me spell it out. You, Mr. Smarty-pants, are Peter Pan! Well, I know you can't fly, but you can do everything else that Peter Pan could, and even some more! You can use Scratch to do amazing things. Let's dive in!

1.4 Things-That-Must-Not-Be-Done!

Peter Pan is nearly invincible, but even he must be wary of a few things that can hurt bad. I am giving you a list of things you must never do when using Scratch or anything on the Internet.

Never share the account password with anyone. This is a golden rule for every account made on the Internet.

Never Interact with Strangers

Never share personal details with anyone on the Internet. Personal details include your name, contact information such as phone number, and where you live. If you think it is important to share, discuss it with an adult in your house so they can decide if it's essential.

Never close the Scratch application without saving the project (later, I will tell you how to save your progress on Scratch).

Never hide if you experience something on the Internet that makes you uncomfortable. Share with your parents so they can protect you.

We, humans, have our limitations. For example, we cannot fly independently (because humans do not possess the physical requirements needed to fly). So, what could happen if some people tried to fly without using an airplane? They would fall (yikes), which would be a very unpleasant sight. Just like humans, every machine and every application has some limits. Scratch is no exception, so we must be aware of them and not exceed the limitations, or things that can become unreliable.

Never leave the computer unattended and unlocked. Pee breaks are essential, but save your Scratch project and lock the computer before you leave. The last thing you do not want is your younger siblings making a mess or someone shutting down the computer.

Scratch does not have an UNDO feature, so the right idea is to plan. Never start a project without thinking it through. With practice, you will not need to make any changes.

Never be shy of making mistakes. Mistakes are fun because they are easy to remember and help you learn new things.

And the most important thing, because it is the hardest of all: Never give up! Things (like life in general) can be hard sometimes. You will be stuck, but never accept the defeat. If you do not succeed at first, try, try, try again!

The Concept of Give and Take

Have you ever gone to some mall along with your parents or to the grocery store? You must have noticed how your parents hand out money or swipe their cards, and, in exchange, the shopkeeper lets them keep whatever they have gathered. Everything in the world works like this. You have to **give** something to **buy or take** something.

Programming works on the same principles. You write a code/program that gives instructions to the computer. The computer processes and you get a response. In the computer world, what you give to the computer, we call "input," and the response we get is called "output."

Now, here is when things can get confusing, so pay attention, kiddo! Programs are written for someone else to use them (we call them "users"). The user will use the program to do some work, in short, giving input and getting the output. This is how the entire world of the Internet works. This is also how the real world works. For example, talking about cars is made by people working in factories. People buy them and use them to go to work, shop, and have fun, like going to picnics.

You are going to be the Peter Pan of programmers. You are going to create stuff that others can use and have fun and learn new things simultaneously.

Start Scratch

Now let's start Scratch. Below are instructions for you on how to start Scratch.

Click on the Scratch application icon on the desktop. The icon

It looks like this:

Scratch 3
App

Scratch will open up. It will look like this. What a fantastic colorful screen! Do not worry if things on this new screen do not make sense to you right now. We are going to explain each section very soon.

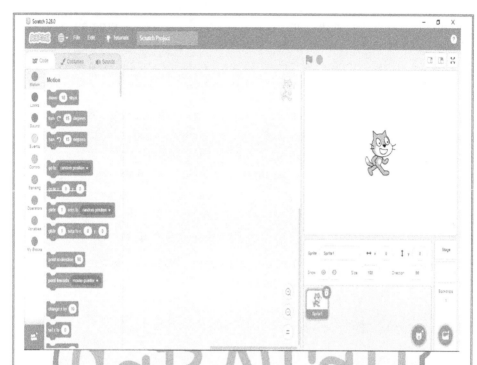

1.6 Understanding Different Sections of the Scratch Screen Menu Bar

The first thing on the Scratch interface you will notice is the blue line at the top with a bunch of options (the bunch of options is called a menu). The blue area is a long and stretched rectangle (like a bar). Hence we call this whole area the menu bar.

The first option in the blue menu bar is the logo of Scratch. Click on it with your mouse, and you will see information about the Scratch application. I see this:

The second option on the menu, represented by the icon of the world, is the "language" used in the Scratch application. You can change language at any time you want. At the start, it is set to English.

- The third option is named "File," to be honest, due to a lack of a better name! This is an option you will find in the menus of almost every application, and it contains general but essential actions. In Scratch, the "File" includes the following options (I will explain these options in a bit).

- The fourth option is "Edit." It has only two options, and we will not be using any of them in this book. However, I will explain to them, just for your curiosity.
- The fifth option is the "Tutorials." You will find projects that you can run to understand different things about Scratch. No need to worry about them, as you have this book!
- The last option is a field where you can name your current project. It might already be filled with "Scratch Project," but you can change it to whatever you like.

"File" Options

Use this option to create a new project. If you have already worked on a current project and have not saved the changes, you will be reminded with a prompt. See, even Scratch knows how forgetful we are!

Load from your Computer: You can load an already saved project using this option. You need to remember where you had saved your project and what the project name was.

Save to your computer: I know how important it is to take a restroom break or eat cookies. You can do both without any worries because you can save your project using this option. Scratch will ask where to save the project and what to name it. Try to save it somewhere you will remember. I usually just select "Desktop." The name you have given to your project is automatically assigned to the filename.

"Edit" Options

Restore: If you have deleted something mistakenly and want it back, you can use this option. Beware that this is not an UNDO button, so it will not revert everything you do in Scratch.

Turn on Turbo Mode: If your project has a lot of complex calculations, activate this mode, and the projects may run faster.

Tabs

You will see three tabs on the Scratch screen like this:

We will learn about the three tabs in greater detail in the next chapters. For now, you should know their purpose.

Code Tab: This is a part of the Scratch interface, where you can find all the blocks you can use to create projects. The blocks are grouped by their type, such as "motion," "looks," and "sound."

Costumes Tab: This tab gives you options to customize the look and behavior of characters in your project.

Sound Tab: If you have used a sound block in your project, here, you will be able to customize each sound component.

Controls

In the same line as the tabs, you will see the following buttons towards the right side of your screen.

Green Flag

This runs your project.

Red Sign

This stops your project from running.

Turbo Mode

You see this if you have enabled the Turbo Mode from the "Edit" option in the menu bar.

View Options

The next three options change the look of the entire Scratch screen.

Stage

This is where you will see how your project runs. Every project starts with the cat character, so that's what we see on the stage.

Sprites and Backdrops

We are going to learn two new words - sprites and backdrops.

Sprites: Sprites are objects that you can add to your object. The blocks we choose from the code tab are applied to these sprites.

Backdrop: Backdrop is your project's background. These are the backgrounds we can choose for our projects.

Chapter 2: The Scratch Interface

The Scratch interface is designed from the left-hand pane to the right; everything needed to create a Scratch project is made available in its interface. On the left pane, the interfaces are grouped and arranged according to the function and task they perform; the motion, looks, sound, pen, control, sensing, operators, and variables. The Scratch interface has been designed in this pattern.

It is essential to mention that the structure of the Scratch interface has made it easier to tinker and explore ideas in Scratch programming. Once projects are created, a user can quickly evaluate the result of the project to determine whether they meet the desired expectations. This is very easy because all the required process is under one interface.

To check the result of a project, a user does not necessarily have to combine codes, switch windows, upload files, or run around any number of possible obstacles or incorrect numbers. Scratch programming makes it easy to modify the program while it is still running and see its outcome.

2.1 Actions and Keyboard Commands

By now, we know how to create and design a Scratch account, a scratch project, and use the scratch editor. We have also learned how to make our Scratch project sprites move, create and use Scratch scripts, and adjust our sprites' movement with the aid of Loops.

Conditional Actions

In Scratch, conditional actions are contingent upon a previous instruction. The blocks used in carrying out these activities are known as the If-Blocks. Below are the steps to carrying out conditional actions in Scratch.

Program Name: Up and Down Steps

Go to the Scratch website and open the homepage. Click on the File/New to create a new Scratch project on the homepage. Using the steps already explained in the previous chapter, name the Project **"Up and Down."**

1. Create and design a script that positions the sprite at the center of the stage. That is the point (0, 0). After this, make the sprite move (10) steps forever 3) Now run your program. As you do this, you will notice that your sprite gets stuck at the right hand side of the stage. It is because Scratch does not permit sprites to leave the scene entirely. To adjust this and make the sprite move up and down the stage, use the next step.

Note: If none of the above mentioned changes happen to your sprite, start your script when the flag clicks block.

2. Inside the if-then block, add a turn counterclockwise 180-degrees block. This script tells Scratch if the x position of the sprite is higher than 240-that is, to determine if it is at the right edge of the stage. Scratch will rotate the sprite to 180 degrees if this is the case. But if it is not, nothing will happen. (If the test condition is false, there is an if-then-else block to rectify this and do something else) In addition to the Repeat Loops that have been explained, if-then and if-then-else blocks are crucial in programming. None of these blocks can be avoided when creating an exciting and educating program.

3. Now rerun the program. Your sprite should move to the edge of the right hand side of the stage, turn around and move it to the left corner of the stage. When you do, the sprite will get stuck again. To rectify this, use the same procedures highlighted above. But in this case, you would add blocks to rotate the sprites 180 degrees if the x position is less than -240.

4. Rerun the program. At this point, your sprite should move continuously between the right and left edges of stage 8. To round up your program, keep your cat's right side up. While you are busy with the commands, you may not have noticed that your cat is upside down when moving to the left edge. However, to avoid flipping back while your program is running, add a set rotation style left-right block from the Motion menu as the first block in your script.

2.2 How to Add More Sprites to a Script

In our explanation of Scratch script and sprite, we mention having more than one script and sprite on the stage area. To demonstrate this, we would explore some of the steps to achieve in this section and explore some additional motion blocks and loops.

Note: there are four ways to add more sprites to our design; they are:

- Paint a new sprite
- Choose a sprite from the library
- Upload a sprite from the file
- A new sprite from the camera

In this part of the book, we will be focusing on adding more sprites from the sprite library. As we progress in the book, we will be exploring all the other sections. This screenshot shows how the sprite library looks like:

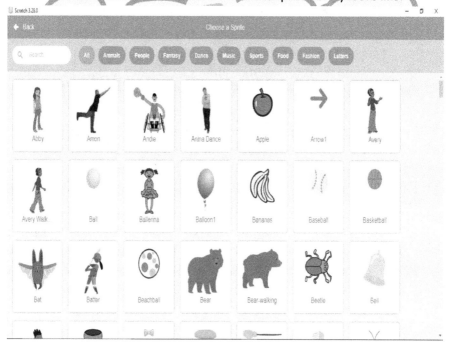

1. Add a new sprite from the library option by clicking on the choose new sprite.
2. We have sprites like the lightning and others on the choose new sprite section. But since the sprite we have been using so far is an animal, it is better to continue this process. Browse and search for the animal section and select Dog1. Click on OK to add the dog to the option.
3. Ensure that you select Dog1 from the sprite list to ensure a sprite area for the dog.
4. Go to the Motion palette and drag one of the turn blocks into the script area.

Note: There are two types of Motion palettes. One of the turn blocks has a circular area that points clockwise, while the other turn block points counterclockwise. The turning block we are using in this project is the one pointing clockwise.

Chapter 3: Creating First Animation

So far, we have extensively explained how to create a Scratch project and how to develop sprites and scripts for our project. We have also assessed some sample scripts and the processes involved in creating animation.

3.1 How to Create your First Animated Card with Scratch Programming

The section will cover:

- How to design a bitmap or vector image by using the built-in paint editor
- How to initialize the starting point of a sprite
- How to compose a simple name for a sprite
- How to design a Happy Birthday Sprite

The very first step of creating an animation is to add the characters. Hence, the first thing we would be learning in this section is how to add a **Happy Birthday** test for our project.

- Click on the Create button on the website.
- Delete the cat sprite by right-clicking on the cat icon, labeled as Sprite1 in the sprites list, and choosing delete.
- After deleting the cat sprite, we would draw a new one by clicking on the Paint new sprite icon.
- Click on the Paint new sprite icon, create a new sprite, and name Sprite1. After this, open the paint editor to an empty canvas. This process is displayed in the screenshot:

- Click on your canvas with the mouse where you want to type. Go ahead and type Happy Birthday.
- If you are not too comfortable with the default font, it can be changed. Highlight your text and look at the bottom of the paint editor to find the Font menu.

- From the picture above, a color palette is displayed. We can use this to change the text color into the color of our choice. To do this, highlight your text and click on your choicest color. Your text will be displayed in the color you choose.
- When you are okay with the words, font, and color, you can save your Sprite by clicking anywhere around the stage area or the paint editor.

The Sprite would be visible on the Stage. However, it is advisable to cross-check your program very well before clicking out of the Text tool. You need to do this because you will not be able to change your text afterwards.

How to Erase Errors

The Scratch toolbar contains an erase tool with an adjustable eraser width to remove some parts of your image. If you want to change or shift the font, color, or words of the text you just created, you can erase the Sprite and start over.

Can you Mess up with the Size of a Bitmap Sprite?

While we save the image we just created, it is noteworthy that Scratch 2.0 does not provide a sprite size setting in its bitmap editing tool. As a result, we would be resizing our image manually.

- If you want to resize the Sprite, click on the grow button and then click on the Sprite.
- Sprite can also be resized by adding the set size to () block from the "Looks" palette.

Drawing with the Vector Image Tool

The above "happy birthday" sprite was created with the bitmap tool. To fully understand the differences between vector image and bitmap tool, we would also be recreating the same Sprite with the vector tool. After this, we would try to resize the Sprite in vector mode.

- Go to the Paint new sprite icon to create a new sprite.
- If you are not in vector mode, convert your image to the vector by simply clicking on the "convert to vector" button at the bottom-right of the editor. When the model changes, the toolbar moves to the right side of the editor.
- Use the text tool in the toolbar to create a **Happy Birthday** sprite.
- To make the Sprite bigger, go to the "Look" palette drag the set size to () block into the Scripts area. Change the size attribute to 300 and click on the block to apply the size.

- Use the above step for the other Sprite we have created to view your project on your computer screen, click on the blue square located at the top of the Stage, to the left of the project name. The display of your Sprite would be similar to this:

- When the Sprite pops up on your screen, the image would be identical to this:

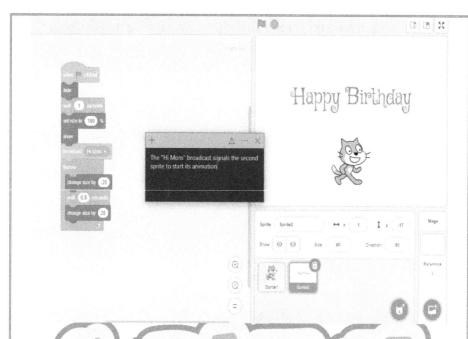

How does a Gradient Work?

You apply colors to the animation, stick around the Stage. As you do, you would notice the first color is darkest at the point where you click onto your Stage, and it gradually fades into the other color.

In gradient, we have three options. The first is the vertical gradient. This usually starts with the primary color at the top of the Stage and gradually fades into the second color. The second is the horizontal gradient. This begins with the first color to the left of the Stage and transitions to the second color as it fills to the right of the Stage. We can use the flip left-right and flip up-down options in the paint editor to change how this works. The third and the last is the circular gradient. This starts wherever you click on the Stage with color one and transitions to the second color as the circle reaches the edge of the Stage.

The gradient works so that it fills a boundary created by another line or shape. But if the Stage is empty, the gradient will fill the entire space. If a square shape is drawn in the center of the Stage, the gradient will restrict itself to just the square's boundary.

How to Add More Sprite to Our Sprite

- Go to the Paint new sprite option and use the Sprite to create the name letters if the person is receiving a card. Create the letters one after the other. For this card, I am sending it to my mom, so I will spell the word "MOM" on the card.
- When you have added the necessary sprites for the name, you can reposition this by clicking and dragging each letter around the Stage to form a word. If the letters are too small, you can resize them as needed.

Adding Comments to the Script

- Select the Happy Birthday script. Right-click somewhere in the scripts area and select "Add comment."
- In the yellow box that appears, type the following: the "hi mom" broadcast signals the second sprite to start its animation
- Click on the yellow comment box and drag it to the broadcast (hi mom) block. Then, release the block. This process would attach the comment to the block. The screenshot below shows how it works:

How to Transform Sprite

In this part of the book, we will be focusing on the Sprite we use to spell the mom and use the graphical complex.

We will add the when I receive () block to the scripts area for Second M.

We will transform the M using the mosaic effect and a repeat loop. To do this,

- Go to the Control palette and drag the repeat () block to the bottom of the show block and change the value to 25.
- Go to the palette, add the change () effect by () block to the repeat loop — select mosaic from the drop-down list to change the effect from the color to mosaic.
- Click on the green flag to see the outcome of our exercise. As you would notice, the M is no longer readable. Click on "Stop" button to continue the program.

- Go to the Looks palette, double-click on the "clear graphic effects" block to redisplay the letter m. This process can also be run by clicking on the name block.
- Drag another repeat () block to the bottom of the first repeat () block and set the value to 25. 9. Insert a second change () effect by () block into the new repeat ten blocks.

Graphical Transformation

The look of your Sprite can be changed, as shown in the screenshot below. The effect in the table after the screenshot can be found in the change () effect by () and set the () effect to () blocks in the Looks palette.

Color: It changes the color of the Sprite. A sprite can have more than 100 color effects. During the process of creating visual art, this effect visually makes out a different state.

Fisheye: This effect alters the edges of the Sprite when you are looking at it through a glass door or peephole - To change the outlook of a sprite For using as a transition effect.

Whirl: Twisting the Sprite around a center point is very similar to throwing a pebble in the water. The larger the whirl effect, the harder it is to see. It is used:

- To alter the sprite movement

- As a transition effect

- To create a spin

 Pixelate: Pixelate increases the size of the pixels so that it is clearer. However, this effect blurs an image. It is used:

- To blur an image

- For the transition effect

- To cover up another sprite

 Mosaic: Mosaic splits the Sprite such that it creates smaller images of itself. It is used:

- For the transition effect

- To split a single sprite into multiple

Brightness: It is used to increase the brightness of the Sprite.

- To make a sprite sparkle

- To make a sprite dimmer

Ghost: This effect makes the Sprite very light and transparent such that one can see other sprites and backgrounds through the Sprite. For instance, a value of 100 hides the Sprite by making it completely transparent; -100 shows the Sprite.

- To hide a sprite

- To create a fade in/out effect in a sprite

- To create transparency similar to a ghost

Brief Explanation

In the above screenshot, the result of the first row is normal, color, fisheye, and whirl. The effects on the second row are pixelated, mosaic, brightness, and ghost. This graphical effect can be reversed by clicking on the clear graphic effect block. This can also be achieved by counteracting the original effect. For instance, if the fisheye effect is set to 100 to derive the above result, this can be reversed by applying a fisheye effect of -100.

In this chapter, we have made our first animated project. In creating the animated birthday card, we were introduced to various Scratch programming concepts. We started creating the Sprite by first using the built-in paint editor to create sprites and examine the differences between vector graphics and bitmap. After this, we animated the script further by using graphical transformations. All through the chapter, the blocks below are part of those we used to make our animation perfect. These blocks include: forever, repeat (), broadcast (), and wait () secs.

3.2 Creating your First Game

In this part of the book, you will create your very first Game. It will be a simple one to get familiar with the interface.

We will explore the basic actions you perform with the editing mode.

Your First Project

We will get hands-on experience, do not worry if you do not understand every step explained in this section; the idea is to get something to work.

In later chapter, we will go through every aspect of block programming, what each element do, and how to make your very own projects.

What is a Project

Projects are animations, stories, art, and games; in other words, just about anything you can make in Scratch.

Create a New Project

To create a new project, find the button 'Create' on the top left side of the home page:

Click Create, and you will be redirected to Scratch Editor Interface.

3.3 The Scratch Editor Interface

The Scratch interface is divided into three sections:

- The Block Palette
- The Script Area
- The Stage

Block Palette: On the left of the Scratch interface is the Block Palette. You can find all the building blocks to create a program.

Script Area: Your script area is in the middle. This is where the building blocks will be added to form your program.

Make your first Game

Let's get to it. You are now in the Scratch Editor Interface. First, you will give the project a name, then make the Cat character move and say something.

Name your Project

To name your project,

- Simply click in the middle box on the top, which currently shows 'Untitled.'
- Enter a name; let's name it "My First Game."
- Then, press Enter on your keyboard for the name to save. The title is now saved.

Make the Cat Move

To make the Cat move, we need to add a Motion block to make the character move and an Event Block to trigger the motion when the Green Flag is clicked.

Move Block

Let's add the motion block first; then, we will add the event.

Add the "Move 10 steps" block. To do this, simply click on the Motion button on the very left of the Blocks Palette, then drag the move ten steps block into the Script Area.

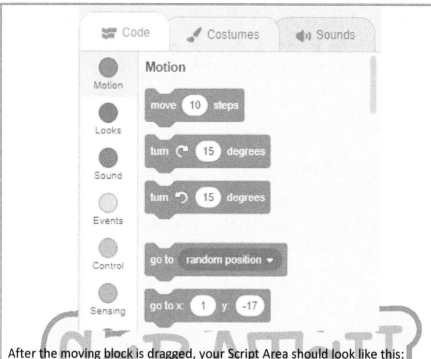

After the moving block is dragged, your Script Area should look like this:

Event Block

We still need to connect it to some Event block to trigger the move. So let's click on the Event button from the Block palette.

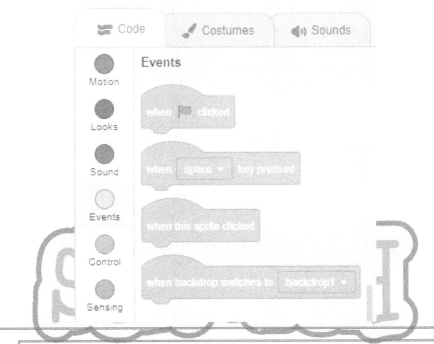

- Drag the When Flag Clicked block above the moving block in the Scripting Area,
- Make sure to connect "When the Flag is Clicked."
- Block right above the moving block:

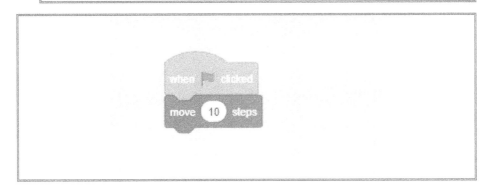

Test

- Your very first game is done. It is quite basic, but see that the Cat character can now move. To test, just click the Green Flag button in the Stage Area.
- You should see the Cat move ten small steps to the right.
- It is a rather small movement, so let's make this a bit more visible by increasing the steps and getting the Cat to return to the original position when you stop the Game.

Note: Scratch projects do not reset any object position when the Game is stopped, so it is always good to move it back to where it was.

Move More

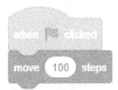

- In the Scripting Area, click on the moving block, where the number 10 is displayed, and type a more significant number, let's say 100:
- Then, click the Green Flag again, and see that the Cat is moving further to the right.
- You have just created a stepped move for your Sprite.

Reset Position

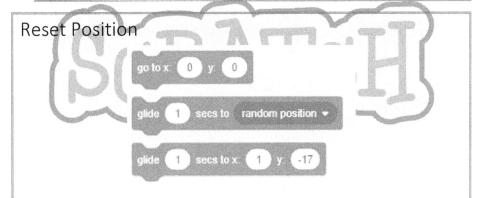

If you click many times on the Green Flag, you will see that the Cat keeps moving to the right, even if you click the Red button to stop your Game. To solve this, let's reset the Cat position when an event occurs. We can trigger events with a keypress; let's try that.

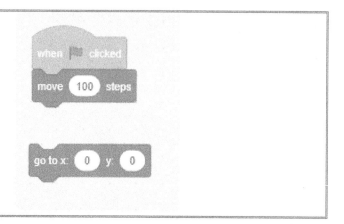

- Find the Event block, called go to x: ( ) y: ( ).
- Drag it into the Scripting Area. Do not connect it to the other two blocks you have placed earlier.
- Now, find the Event block, called "when the space key pressed."
- And drag it into the Scripting Area, plugging it above the go to x y block. Ensure that the go-to x y block has 0 for x and 0 for y.

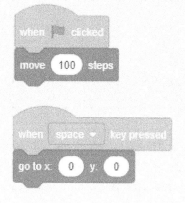

- Now click the green flag button, then press the space key on your keyboard to see that the Cat is moving back to the center of the Stage.
- Try again clicking the Green flag button a few times and see that hitting the space key always puts the Cat back in the middle of the Stage.

Make the Cat Say Something

Now we will make the Cat talk. You will make it say something after he finishes moving.

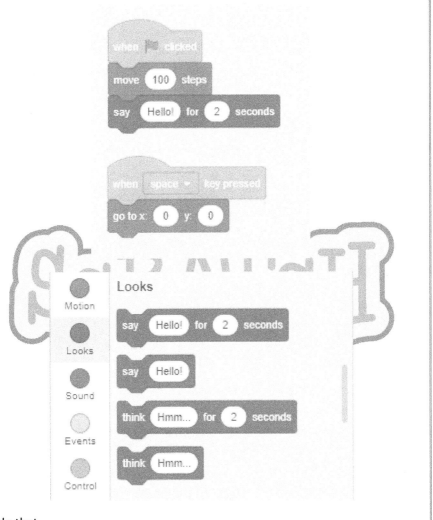

To do that,

- Find the Look block called Say Hello for 2 Seconds.
- And drag it into the Scripting Area. Plug it below the move 100 steps block.
- Now test it, by clicking the Green Flag button on the Stage area.

- You should see the Cat first move to the right, then Say Hello for 2 seconds.

Tweak your First Game

Let's change a few things.

You can click on the say hello for 2 seconds block in your Scripting area and change the word Hello to anything you want, for example, Greetings!

You can also change the number of seconds the Cat talks; make it say something for 5 seconds instead. Or even add another block to make it say something else for a few seconds after the Cat said something.

Save your Game

You would not want to lose your Game, so make sure to save your project from time to time.

To do so, click on File -> Save now on the top left of the screen.

Your project is now saved. If you leave the Scratch platform and come back later, you will be able to play, see and edit your saved Game.

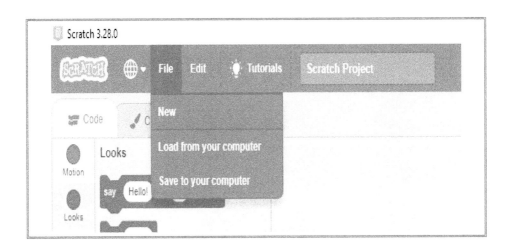

Chapter 4: Learning Important Concepts through Developing Games

4.1 Building Lego

Let us see how we build something using a Lego set.

Let's create a list of everything we need.

- A complete Lego set. We will not be able to build the desired construction if parts are missing entirely.
- A picture of the completed construction. This helps us know if we have put everything together in the right way.

The Lego set also comes with instructions and the sequence on building using that set. You must follow the instructions in the correct sequence to complete the build. Here is a step-by-step guide on how to build something using a Lego set.

- Identify all the different pieces (we also call them bricks).
- If there are too many bricks, divide them into several heaps by grouping similar bricks together.
- Using the instructions, start building in the given sequence. I know skipping a few steps sounds tempting, but do not skip a step. It will make things difficult down the line.
- Once the construction is built, pose like a king because you truly deserve it, and maybe some pizza!

Using Scratch to build stuff is similar to building things with Lego sets. In both situations, it is essential to follow the sequence.

Here's some Gandalf wisdom for you: Shortcuts are never good, not in real-life and not while programming. If you do not know who Gandalf is, well, that needs to be corrected right away!

He's the most powerful wizard in this world and beyond.

Having Fun with Blocks

Are you still confused about the difference between scripts and blocks?

<u>Blocks</u> are instructions for characters to follow. You can make the actors move, dance, and even scream using blocks.

When you have blocks joined together, it forms a **Script**. The Script of your movie

Ah! Now you get it. Actors, Directions, Scripts, and Stage. It is all about making movies.

But how will you remember all these blocks?

You do not need to remember any blocks. Just try them out and learn how each one works. You must be feeling a little comfortable with Scratch now.

Fun with Colors

I love the colors. Movies are full of colors.

Jumpy, can you even see all colors?

Frogs can see colors. We also have a 360 degrees vision. **BAAM!**

But you don't have flexible necks, HA HA HA! We don't need one. HU HU HU!

I will show you how the color blocks work in Scratch in this project. You can then make colorful movies. The name of our project is "Fun color."

Step 1: Open Scratch. Opening Scratch will always be your first step.

Step 2: To add Events blocks, go to Events blocks (brown color) and drag the "When space key pressed" block to the scripts area.

Why not the Green Flag Again?

Instead of the green flag, we will use the space bar on your keyboard to start the movie.

But, if you want, you can also use the green flag.

As a Director, you can start your movie in different ways like a green flag, space bar, click, sound, and more.

Step 3: The Forever block From the Control (orange color) section (or palette), drag the forever block to the scripts working area and snap it to the When - space block.

A Forever block goes on and on forever like the Earth. Jumpy is forever confused.

How do I Stop the forever block?

Good question, Jumpy. You can stop the forever block by clicking the RED STOP button.

Step 4: Changing the color Go to the Looks section of the Scripts palette and then drag "Change color effect by 25" block.

To the Scripts area and snap it to the forever block.

Because you want to change the looks of your actor, you have to go to the Looks section of the Scripts palette.

The Looks section includes blocks that change the actor's looks and make them speak.

These blocks include say, think, hide, switch costumes, set color, and more. Press the SPACE bar on your keyboard to see the color of the cat change very fast.

Jumpy, do you know how to start this movie?

Of course. Press the **SPACE** bar. Fast, I think you are not paying attention to the details.

Jumpy thought I was sleeping, but I was just pulling his leg.

I love to be creative. Can I try to hide and show my actor forever? Yes, you can. That is precisely what the next step is about.

Step 5: Hide and Show from the Looks section, drag and drop the show and hide blocks into the scripts area. Snap them inside the forever block.

My cat disappeared when I pressed the space bar. Did I do something wrong?

Jumpy, you forgot something from the first chapter. Because the actor changes so fast, you stop seeing the actor.

We covered a little bit in the first chapter, but you do not have to reread it.

Is it the wait block?

Exactly! You got it right.

Wait block is used in many programs to slow the actor's speed.

Step 6: The Wait block From the Control section, drag two wait blocks onto the scripts area.

Snap the first wait block before the show and the second before the hidden block.

Step 7: Running the movie - **Now, run the movie!**

You will see the cat blink and change colors.

4.2 Rock Paper Scissors

The first thing that we need when creating a game is brainstorming. Take a pen and paper and think about how the game should be designed. Start by first considering the game's rules, and only then worry about the programming side.

This classic game involves choosing one of three objects, as the name suggests. Once both selections are made, the items are revealed to see who wins. Three simple rules determine the player who wins. The rock will crush the scissors, cut paper, and the paper cover the rock.

To handle these rules, we will create a list of choices, similar to the list of colors we created before in some of our drawing programs. Then we will add a random selection function that will represent the choice the computer makes. Next, the human player will have to make their choice. Finally, the winner is decided with the help of several if statements.

Before we continue with the code, you should start performing these steps independently. You already have the plan, and know which steps you need to take. So, simply break down the game into manageable sections and work on one at a time.

Have you tried to create your version of the game yet? If so, good job! Even if you have not finished it or you have written the game but you are getting some errors, you should still reward yourself for trying. Now, let's go through the code and see how this game should turn out: import random

```
selectionChoices = [ "rock", "paper", "scissors"]

print ("Rock beats scissors. Scissors cut paper. Paper covers rock.")

player = input ("Do you want to choose rock, paper, or scissors? (or quit) ?"
while player != "quit":

    player = player.lower ()

computer = random.choice(selectionChoices) print("You selected " +player+ ",
and the computer selected" +computer+ ".") if player == computer:
                    print("Draw!")

            elif player == "rock":
        if computer == "scissors": print ("Victory!")

                    else:

                print("You lose!")

            elif player == "paper":
    if computer == "rock": print("Victory!") else: print("You lose!")

        elif player == "scissors": if computer == "paper":

        print ("Victory!") else: print("You lose!") else:

            print("Something went wrong...") print()

player = input ("Do you want to choose rock, paper, or scissors? (or quit) ?"
```

First, we import the random package, which allows us to use several functions that we will take advantage of when giving the computer the ability to make random choices. Then we create a list for the three-game objects and print the game's rules so that the human player knows them. After all, the computer will already know what to do because it is programmed. Next, we ask the player to type their choice, and then a loop is executed to check the player's choice. The player also can quit the prompt window, and when that happens, the game is over. Our loop makes sure that if the player doesn't select the quit option, the game will run.

The next step is to ask the computer to select one of the three-game objects. This choice is made randomly, and the selected item is stored inside a variable called "computer." After memorizing the choice, the testing phase begins to see which player will win. A check is performed to check whether the two players have chosen the same item. If they have done, the result is a draw, and nobody wins. Next, the program verifies whether the player chose rock, and then it looks at the computer to see if it chose scissors. If this is the case, the rule says rock beats scissors, so the player wins. If the computer does not select a rock, neither does it pick scissors, then it has certainly chosen paper. In this case, the computer will win. Next, we have two elif statements where we perform two more tests that check whether the player has selected paper or scissors. Here we also have a statement that checks whether the player has chosen something that is not one of the three possible items. Some error message is sent that tells the player that he has chosen something that he is not allowed or mistyped the command.

Lastly, the user is prompted to type the next selection. This is where the main loop goes back to the beginning. In other words, the game starts another round of rock paper scissors.

This game is simple, but it is fun because anyone can win. The computer has a chance of beating you, and there's also a real chance of ending up in a draw. Now that you understand how to create a random chance type.

Let's look at other examples to add to our game library while also learning Python programming.

Guess!

This project will be another fun chance-based game that will use the random module. The game's purpose will be to choose a number between a minimum and a maximum, and then the opponent tries to guess that number. If the player guesses a higher number, he will have to try a smaller one and the other way around. Only a perfect match will turn into a win.

The random module is needed in this project because of certain specific functions. For instance, we know that we need to generate a random number. Therefore we will use a function called "randint" which stands for random integer. The function will have two parameters, which represent the minimum number we can have and the maximum. You can try out this function on its own. Just import the module and then type the following: import random

random.randint (1, 20)

Python will now automatically generate a random figure between 1 and 20. Remember that the minimum and maximum values are included in the number generation. Therefore, Python can also generate numbers 1 to 20. You can test this command as many times as you want to ensure that you are truly getting random values. If you execute it often enough, you will see that some values will repeat themselves, and if the range is large enough, you might not even encounter certain numbers no matter how many times you run the code. Interestingly, though, this function is that it is not truly random. This is just a side note that will not affect your program, but it is intriguing, nonetheless. The randint function follows a specific pattern, and the chosen numbers only appear to be random, but they are not. Python follows a complex algorithm for this pattern instead, and therefore, we experience the illusion of randomness. With that being said, let's get back to fun and games. Let's create our game with the following code: import random

randomNumbers = random.randint (1, 100)

myGuess = int (input ("Try to guess the number. It can be anywhere from 1 to 100:"))

while guess != randomNumbers:

if myGuess > randomNumbers:

print (myGuess, "was larger than the number. Guess again!" if myGuess < randomNumbers:

```
print (myGuess, "was smaller than the number. Guess again!" myGuess = int
(input ("Try and guess again! "))

print (myGuess, "you got it right! You won!")
```

That's it! Hopefully, you have tried to create this game on your own because you already have the tools for the job. Remember that programming is only easy as long as you practice it enough independently. Just take it one step at a time. With that being said, let's discuss the code in case you need some help figuring the game out:

Just like before, we first need to import the random module to use the random number generating function.

Next, we use the randint function with two parameters. As mentioned before, these parameters are the lowest number we can guess, 1, and the highest number we can guess 100. The random number generator will start generating a number within this range. Once the number is generated, it is stored inside the "randomNumbers" variable, which we have declared. The player will not know this number because they need to guess it. That is the point of the game.

Next, the player needs to guess the hidden number. This guess will then be stored inside a new variable called "myGuess." To check whether the guess equals the number, we are using a while loop with the "not equal to" operator. We do this because if the player gets lucky and guesses the number correctly with the first attempt, the loop simply does not finish executing because there is no need.

Next, if the player guesses the wrong number, we have two if statements that check whether the guess is a higher value than the hidden number or a lower one. An appropriate message is then printed for the player in each case. The player receives another chance to make the right guess in either scenario. Finally, in the end, if the user guesses the number correctly, the program declares victory by printing a message, and then the program stops running.

To make the game more interesting, you can challenge yourself to modify the random number generator to include different values. You can also add a statement that enables the game to print the score to see how many times the player has tried to guess the number. Besides, since the game ends when the player guesses, you could write the main loop to choose to restart the game instead of automatically quitting. Have fun, and do not be afraid to try anything.

4.3 Choose a Card

Card games are always fun, and they also rely on random elements to some degree. No matter the card game, chances are quite small to have multiple identical games. This means you will not get bored any time soon. We can create a card game with what we have discussed so far about Python programming. It might not look good unless you have an artistic friend to draw everything for you, but you could still create the graphics with the help of the Turtle module like we did for other projects. This will require some patience, though. In any case, we can create a card game even without graphics by merely generating the name of each card. Instead of seeing a virtual card, we will see the name "four of spades" or "queen of hearts."

Before we move further, you should note that this project is your challenge. You have now learned everything you need to write such a game, and we have already created two other similar projects. So this time, you are almost entirely on your own. As usual, start with a pen and paper and figure everything out logically. Worry about the code afterward. However, to help you out a little, we will brainstorm together just to give you some ideas.

One of the simplest card games we could create involves two players who battle each other to see who draws the card with the highest value. Each player will randomly pull a card from the deck, and the one who has the higher card will win. It is a simple game but fun due to the element of randomness.

Since we will not be using any graphics, we will have to create our deck of cards somehow. We will set them all up as a list of strings since we will be using their names instead. Next, we need to give the players the ability to randomly pull a card from the deck. This means that we will use the random module once again, and we will add a choice function that randomly distributes cards to the players. Finally, we need a way to compare the two cards drawn by the two players. As you probably have guessed, this is a case for comparison operators.

That is pretty much all it takes to create a card game. You can add more features or remove some if you are not interested in them. Whatever you do, design the game on paper to know your goals. Then work on one line of code at a time. This way, you will write your game in no time, and whatever problems you encounter, you will be able to fix quite quickly.

4.4 Merry Go Round

Have you been to a circus or a local festival where they have rides and things for everyone? Or you might have seen one on TV. The fancier merry-go-rounds have horse rides that also move up and down.

In programming, we also have things that go round, round, and round! They are called loops. Yes, just loops, not the front loops everyone loves! With loops, we can do one or more tasks several times.

There are essentially two types of loops:

Loops run a specific number of times. We set the counter when creating the loop.

Loops that run until a specific condition is met. We define that condition when creating the loop.

We are going to work on two projects in this chapter. Each project will focus on one type of loop.

Loop #1

Have you ever taken a ride in a helicopter? Helicopters are so cool and scary at the same time. I loved helicopters. I had never flown on a helicopter, but I used to be a helicopter enthusiast as a kid. I used to collect helicopter models and read books about them. I remember, I was inspired by the 80s TV show Airwolf. Ok, let me be clear it. I am not that old, and there's nothing wrong with watching ancient TV shows, especially when they are as unique as Airwolf.

Do you know what's even cooler than helicopters? Spaceships! The first time I saw a spaceship was in a movie. I do not remember what the movie's name was, but it made a lasting impression on me. Well, not everyone can go on spaceships. Technology is still not that advanced! But, that does not mean we cannot imagine hopping onto a spaceship and cruising along the surface of an alien planet. You know what, let's do that!

- Create a new project and name it "Third Project."

- Add a backdrop named "Space."
- Add a "Rocketship" sprite. Make sure it is selected in the "sprite and backdrop" section and change the direction of the sprite to 139:
- Now, making sure the "Rocketship" sprite is still selected, start adding the following blocks (in the same order):
- Add "when clicked" block from the "Events" options in the Code tab.
- Add "go to x:124 y:107" block from the "Motion" options in the Code tab. Change the x value to -176 and the y value to 107.
- Now, from "Control" options in the same Code tab, add the block that looks like this (change the 10 to 70):
- Inside the jaw of the above loop block, place a "change x by 10" block, which is found in the "Motion" options in the Code tab. Change the 10 to 8.
- From the "Sound" options in the Code tab, drag the "start sound **space ripple**" and place it inside the loop block after the motion block.

The final stack will look like the image below.

The stage may look like this before running the project:

Now, run your project by clicking on the green flag and see the spaceship speed through the night sky of this alien planet with very mysterious sci-fi sound effects!

Loop #2

The loop we have used in the previous project will run 70 times because we have set that value in the loop. What if we do not know the exact number when creating the loop? For example, if you run the above project, you will see that the spaceship flies off the screen. What if we want to run the loop until our sprite touches the edge of the stage?

Let's see how we can do that. Let me introduce my health-conscious friend, Avery, who needs our guidance while walking around the city streets. Let's create a fun little project to help Avery walk on city streets without wandering out too far.

Let's create a new project. If the previous project is still open, save it before creating a new project. Name the new project, "Fourth Project" and start making the following changes.

- Choose the "Colorful City" backdrop.
- Select the "Avery Walking" sprite. Change the size to 40. Change the x and y values to x: -220 and y: -123. The sprite setting should look like this.

Now, we need to add some blocks to this Avery.

- Add "point in direction 90" block from the "Motion" options in the Code tab.
- Add "go to x:124 y:107" block from the "Motion" options in the Code tab. Change the x value to -213 and the y value to -123.
- Now, add the block from the "Control" options in the same Code tab.
- In the hollow box of this loop block, put the block "touching MOUSE-POINTER" block. Change MOUSE-POINTER to EDGE.
- Inside the same loop block, add a "change x by 10" block from "Motion" options under the Code block. Change 10 to 2.

The block stack should look like this.

Now, we need to duplicate this whole block.

- Right-click on this and select "Duplicate." It will create another block stack.
- Place it anywhere on the workspace with a left-click. We need to change the settings on the second stack like below:

- Change "point in direction 90" to -90
- Change "go to x: -213 y: -123" to 216 and -123 Change "change x by 2" to -2
- After the stacks are adjusted, put "when clicked" block from the "Events" options in the Code tab at the top of the entire stack.

When you are done, the entire stack will look like this:

This whole stack will help Avery move from one end of the street to the other, turn around and then walk to the street end she started from. It is a very cool project. Save it with the name "Fourth Project" so you can help Avery whenever needed.

A Loop within a Loop

Let's help Avery again because she wants to make at least ten rounds on the street. Do not blame her; she wants to be healthy! We need to add one loop block to our Fourth Project, and Avery can walk up and down the city street.

We will use the loop#1 type and wrap most of the blocks inside them, as shown in the image below. We will use five as the number of times the loop will execute.

4.5 Cartoons Are Cool

We will start with step-by-step instructions on how you can create a short animation titled Max and Cheesy - our very own tribute to the famous Tom and Jerry cartoons. You will replicate the steps and watch the animation with friends and family.

- Create a new project and name it "Seventh Project."
- Add a cat sprite, rename it Max and give it x and y values of -184 and -122.

We will use an extension to add sound effects to our animation. On the bottom left corner of the Scratch screen, you will see a unique icon with a plus sign. With this option, we can add advanced extensions that help create animations and games.

Choose the first option of "text to speech." This extension adds some blocks that will help us convert text into speech. We can also add background music to our animation.

We will add the following three sprites to our project:

Cat, rename it to Max.

Mouse, rename it to Cheesy.

Puppy, rename it to Rocky.

We can take advantage of the huge library available directly through Scratch. When Max is selected, go to the "Sounds" tab. Towards the bottom-left corner of the screen, you will see the following icon. Click on the search icon, and you will see a catalog of sounds.

- Click on the "Loop" and select the "Mystery" music.
- Let's go back to the Code tab and start using the blocks.
- Select the Max sprite and add the blocks in the following order.

The "set voice to tenor" and "set language to English" will be available under the "Text to Speech" option of the Code tab.

The next stack for Max is given below.

The only new thing we have used in this stack is the broadcast block. It is present in the "Events" option under the Code tab. The purpose of the broadcast is to transfer control to another sprite. The remaining blocks for Max are given below.

Note how they speak and say blocks are grouped to create a subtitles effect in the speech. The last block stack for Max is.

The last three blocks end the execution of the entire project.

The blocks for Cheesy are given below. Select Cheesy in the "sprites and backdrop" area and create the block stack.

The block stack for Rocky is given next.

The last thing to do is to add a backdrop to our project. We have used the "Room 2" backdrop, but you can use something else if you want to.

We have relied heavily on broadcasts to transfer execution flow from one sprite to another. One new "Motion" block used in this project is the "glide." The glide block moves the sprite in a rather smooth fashion instead of jumping it to a specific position (which is what the "go to x: y:" block does). I have used both Motion blocks in this project so that you can note the difference between their usage and results.

The Calculator

Yes, we will create a simple calculator that takes two numbers and performs addition, multiplication, division, and subtraction.

We can start with a new project, naming it "Ninth Project." We do not need a backdrop or sprite, but we can leave the cat sprite as it is; it is up to you.

Here, we are going to use operators with variables. We also use a new input method available in the "Sensing" option under the Code tab.

- We start building the block stack with the "when clicked" block.
- Add "when clicked" block from the "Events" options in the Code tab.
- Create six variables "num1", "num2", "add," "sub," "mul" and "div" using the "create variable" block in the "Variables" option
- Use the ask block from the "Sensing" option to take the first number as input.
- Use the "set" block to store this input to num1 variable Repeat steps 3 and 4 for num2.
- Use the set block for addition. This time, use the addition operator from the "Operators" option under the Code tab with the two variables num1 and num2.
- Repeat step 6 for subtraction, multiplication, and division, each time choosing the relevant operator with the set block.
- In the "Variables" option, make sure num1 and num2 are unchecked while the remaining four variables are checked to show on the stage.
- Our calculator is ready.

It is a fully functional calculator. Can you add any new features to this calculator? You may add more operations such as logical operators (comparison, etc.) or add a loop, so the user keeps using a calculator until they press a specific keyboard key. Take it as the next challenge.

The first program I wrote was in BASIC language, and it was a simple calculator. I had to add a lot of code to handle zero issues and other problems in the division. Try division by zero on your new Scratch calculator. See if it breaks the calculator, or you get answers that make sense. Also, try very large numbers and very small numbers. Check the performance of the calculator. If you want to test the capacity and capability of a project, you need to throw things at it that no one ever thought about. After building a project, your aim should be to try and do everything to break it. It will make your thought process even more creative. You will think of stuff you didn't think about when creating the project.

4.6 Balloon Popper

You must have popped balloons at a birthday party. It is exciting, scary, and fun at the same time. In this project, you will create a game where the balloons are falling from above, and you have to pop the balloons before they pass the bottom of the screen. There is a one-minute timer, and the game will stop after it is over. Each balloon popped will add 10 points to the score. There should be constant music playing in the background. A pop sound should be played when a balloon is popped.

There are no levels, so balloons will always fall at the same speed, and the timer is always set to one minute. It is a more fun game when challenging your friends, taking turns. Whoever scores the most points, will win.

Cheese Wheel

Guide Marty, the mouse, to the cheese wheel. Players start with three lives. The player should use the arrow keys to guide the mouse to the cheese without touching the sides of the tunnels. The tunnel walls are laced with poison, and touching the tunnel wall once will decrease lives by one.

There will be three levels of the game. There must be a new tunnel map at each level, each harder than the previous one. The size of the mouse will also increase by 10 for added difficulty.

Minesweeper

Microsoft Windows used to come with a very cool game called Minesweeper. Unfortunately, Windows 10 does not have it anymore. The good thing is, we can create a minesweeper using Scratch. How is the game played? Well, the game starts with square cells, each with hidden content. You need to click on a cell to reveal its content. Some cells contain a mine. If you click on a cell and it reveals a mine, the game is over. Revealing each cell without touching a mine adds to your total score. You need to reveal all cells in a specific amount of time. Each cell has a number, which tells how many mines there are in its neighborhood. Note that a square can have nine neighbors at maximum.

This might not look like this, but this game is thrilling and fun. There's also a timer so you can see how much time it took for you to clear the field. The timer does not affect the outcome; it is just for bragging rights.

There will be three difficulty levels chosen at the start of the game. Each level has a more significant field and more mines. On the other hand, clearing each cell with greater difficulty gets you more points. When one difficult level is completed, the player should be asked to continue to the next level.

To place mines randomly on the field, you can use the randomizer block available in Scratch.

Above mentioned projects have varying difficulties in terms of building. If you are not able to complete them, do not be discouraged. You can find many project ideas on the Scratch website. Focus on that, and once you are ready, come back to these.

Ball Game

In this example, we will try to create a single-player game. The game isn't complicated, and its purpose is to make players move a paddle to keep the tennis ball from hitting the floor. As you can suggest, the game we will try to make using Scratch is based on the classic game that many of us have played as children, Pong's arcade game.

The concept is simple; the ball starts at the top of the stage pane and moves down. The angle of the ball's movement is random, which means that it can bounce off the edges of the stage on its way toward the bottom of the display. The player's role is to move the paddle using the mouse and send the ball back up. The paddle moves horizontally, and if the player fails to send the ball up and it touches the stage, the game ends. Of course, we will need several steps to create the game, but first, we need to open a new Project and remove a cat-shaped sprite. You can do that by selecting "file 4new" on the Scratch menu, and the new project will open. Cat sprite is deleted by selecting" delete" from the drop menu once you right-click on it.

The first step is to prepare the backdrop. If you want to command the game to recognize when the ball missed the paddle, you will need to mark the bottom of the stage pane with a color of your choice. The preferred color can be selected from the sensing category, and then you can apply it to the block, which will detect if the ball touched the color during the game or not. When you finish this, click once again on the stage to return to it and then go again to the backdrops tab. Use the drawing option to draw a thin rectangle (that resembles a paddle) that will be positioned at the bottom of the backdrop.

The next step is to try adding the paddle and the ball. To do this, you need to add the paddle sprite to your project first. Click on the "new sprite" button that appears above the sprite list. The paddle is a thin rectangle like what we mentioned in the first step. That is why you should repeat that step and draw the same rectangle representing the paddle. You can color the paddle once you finish it using any color that you want while setting the center at the approximate middle of the rectangle. You should name the sprite with something that will explain its function. In this case, the most logical name of the sprite that you added is "paddle." This image should have its y coordinate set to be 120 in value. Now, you have managed to put a paddle into your game, but you still need a ball that is supposed to bounce through the stage pane. The best way to add the ball is to click on the Scratch library, choose one of the existing sprites, and import it into your game. The dialogue will appear with a category inside when you click the library. Choose that category and select a tennis ball sprite that will immediately be added to the project.

Similarly, as with the paddle name, you can name this new sprite "ball" since that is its primal description and role. To prevent any unpredictable occurrences, you should save the project to your computer before making scripts for the game. You can do that by selecting file downloads and selecting which folder you want to save it. For example, you can name it "pong," and it will appear on your computer as Pong.sb2. If you have made an account and logged in while making the game, you can also save your progress on the Scratch server or the cloud. Regardless of where you want to store your files, keep in mind that the best way to protect your work is to save the things you do as often as you can. Now you have the two most essential sprites for your game.

The step that follows these initial sprites is to decide how the game will start and to make these sprites move. Since you are the game designer, you can choose how players will start their new rounds. For instance, you can make them start the game only if they press a specific key. Also, it can start by clicking at one of the sprites or even clapping if the player has a proper webcam that can be used. Still, in this example, we will use the green flag that you will see above the stage because it is the most popular option in Scratch. The way of making this work is very straightforward. Every Script that starts with this green flag will trigger the block when clicked, and it will run whenever you press that particular button. When the Script starts, the flag becomes bright green, and that color stays until the Script is finished.

So once you click the green flag, you go to the XY block and set the vertical position of the paddle to -120 degrees. You should double-check this before you continue because it can happen that you accidentally move the value with the mouse. The goal is to make the paddle that you have made hover above the rectangle (colored pink, for example) at the bottom of the stage pane. If you have made a thicker rectangle, just adapt its position number to work in your design without problems. When you do all this, the Script will automatically turn to the "forever" block, which will continuously check the mouse's position during the game. Try moving the paddle back and then forth while matching the x position of the mouse with the x position of the paddle. Then try running the Script by clicking the green flag we mentioned before, but try moving your mouse up and down this time. If everything is ok, the paddle should follow the movement of the mouse. When you finish testing this part, click the stop icon next to the green flag and stop the Script.

Another script you need to make is the one for the ball sprite, and it is a little longer than the one you had to make for the paddle. To avoid confusion, we will divide the Script into smaller parts. The first thing that now you need to do is the same as for the paddle, you have to click the green flag above the sprite, and the ball will start moving, which means that now we can add the Script that suits the game. We will move the ball sprite to the upper part of the stage pane and command it to go down at a random angle. You need to pick the random block button marked with V from the operators' category to do this. Like before, the Script automatically uses the forever block (marked with the letter w) and moves the ball all over the stage pane while bouncing it off the edges of the displayed area. Try testing everything you have done so far by clicking the green flag. If you do everything correctly, the ball should be moving using the zigzag pattern, and the paddle you previously scripted should follow the moves you make with the mouse. You can try out replacing values inside the moving block and make the game harder by increasing the number that is inside. When you decide what kind of level you want for your game, just click stop, and then you can continue designing your game.

The next part of the Script that you will need to write is how to make the ball that points down, bounce off the paddle and you can move it with the mouse. It is straightforward if you modify the forever block you have in the previous part of the Script. Adjust the block so the ball can travel up when it hits the paddle. You will do that by commanding the ball that the paddle goes in a random direction when it touches. In this example, we will say that this space should be between -30 and 30 on the Y scale. Now, when the forever block starts running for the next round of the game, the moving block will execute the command, which will cause the ball sprite to travel up. If you want to test this again, click the green flag, and once you make sure that your ball is bouncing off the paddle in the way you expected it to, you can use the stop icon to pause the Script. At this point, the only thing that needs to be coded is ending the game if the paddle does not prevent the ball from touching the bottom of the stage pane. You can add this Script to the ball sprite before or after the previous block that you scripted. The moving block can be found in the sensing category, while the stop block can be found in the control palette. It should work like this:

- You click the mouse over the square that is colored, and the cursor should change from some arrow to the hand.
- Move the hand cursor and click above the pink rectangle that appears at the bottom of the stage, and keep in mind that the square you are using should match the rectangle's color.
- If you click "stop all block," it will execute the action that its name suggests and stop running every Script in every sprite that you have in your project.

This means that neither the ball nor the paddle is an exception. With this, you have your first basic game that is fully functional. Still, you should test it a few more times to ensure that all parts of the game are working properly. If everything is fine, you have achieved one of Scratch's main goals, i.e., to make a complete game using a very small amount of code. These are some of the things that make Scratch more accessible than other programing languages.

The final thing you can do is to make your game more fun with sound. You can do that by adding sound every time you hit the ball with the paddle. The simplest way to add sound is to double-click at the ball sprite on the stage, then select the sounds tab. In the beginning, the best thing is to use some of the sounds from Scratch's library, so you click the "choose a sound from the library" button and then add one of the sounds that you like to add to the sprite by clicking OK. After you finish this, go to the scripts tab again and insert the sound block from the sound category. Keep in mind that you should test the game after this, and if everything is alright, you will hear a sound that you have chosen (a short "pop" sound, for example) every time you touch the ball with the paddle. You have completed your first game using Scratch as the programming language with this final touch. Now, you can always add more features by adding two or more balls; for example, the process is the same, so the only thing you need is the time to explore and experiment further. The following text will be more dedicated to Scratch's types of blocks, and some of those blocks were intensively used to build up the game from our example.

Cat game

Our cat, Mona, is hungry. This project will enable Mona to go near Abby and demand some food! Well, Mona would just say "meow," but Abby will know what Mona wants. We all know what cats want - food!

Let's add Mona and Abby to our "First Project." Here is how to do that.

To rename this project, click on the field beside Tutorials in the menu bar and type in "First Project."

Our cat will already be added to the project. We have to move the cat towards the bottom left side of the stage. On the stage, click and drag on the cat to move it.

In the bottom right corner of your screen, in the "sprites and backdrops" section, hover your mouse on the icon that looks like a cat icon (it will say "Choose a Sprite"), and a blue strip will slide up. Select the first icon from the bottom that looks like a magnifying glass (the icon usually used to say "search").

You will see a popping window with a lot of characters. Select the one that says, "Abby."

In the "sprites and backdrops" section, you will see two sprites.

You will notice that Abby is selected because her icon has a thick blue border. We have to flip her, so she faces toward the west. Click on the "Direction" and change the direction of the arrow so it points toward the west. Also, click on the **"arrowheads"** icon in the middle. I have given before and after images on the next page to avoid any confusion.

Conclusion

Congratulations if you have made it this far! Rejoice, but remember, your journey in the creative world has just started. You can see hundreds of tutorials on Scratch on YouTube from which you can get advanced training. Your time given to Scratch is a significant investment. It will pay off a lot in the future.

And it is not just about the future. How cool will it be when you show your projects to your friends and challenge them to beat you at them? You already know you are so good at it. Yet, everything becomes better when you have others to enjoy it with.

As a parent or guardian to a kid, it is crucial to encourage your kid to take on new challenges. Kids thrive in stressful situations. Now, there's a breaking point for every human. So, you must monitor your kid's progress and make sure they are not pushed beyond their limits. Kids might not understand this fact and will feel frustrated.

This book has been written to help learners understand the process better. Learners have been also shown how to use the instruction blocks related to conditional statements, variables, lists, spring, algorithm, operators, and keyboard input available in Scratch.

Becoming a programmer means that you will have to invest time and patience. However, Scratch allows you to explore, play, and experiment without paying that much attention to codes. Scratch's design has made it user-friendly, and every person in the world can use it regardless of their computer science knowledge. Remember that we have not used the most recent version of Scratch but they all have the same concept, so you will easily find your way around in every Scratch interface you use.

From now onwards, you will do all the efforts to polish your skills and introduce new ideas that will improve the ones you have just learned. So, make sure to practice everything you have just learned, and you will become a good programmer without a doubt. Even if you struggle with some concepts, just break them into more straightforward elements. If you still find yourself in need of help, join one of the countless online programming communities that are beginner-friendly. Learn with others and, above all, have fun because this is a journey to learning future skills. If you have found this book helpful in learning the Scratch, leave a comment on Amazon.

I wish you the best of luck on your journey.